The Parable of the Woman and the Judge

Luke 18:1–8 for children

Written by Claire Miller

Illustrated by Dave Hill

CONCORDIA PUBLISHING HOUSE · SAINT LOUIS

"Come listen to My story,"
Jesus said, "and when it's through,
You'll see how much God loves it
When you pray to Him. It's true!

"My story is about a judge
Who wasn't kind or fair.
He didn't rule by God's Commandments,
And he didn't care."

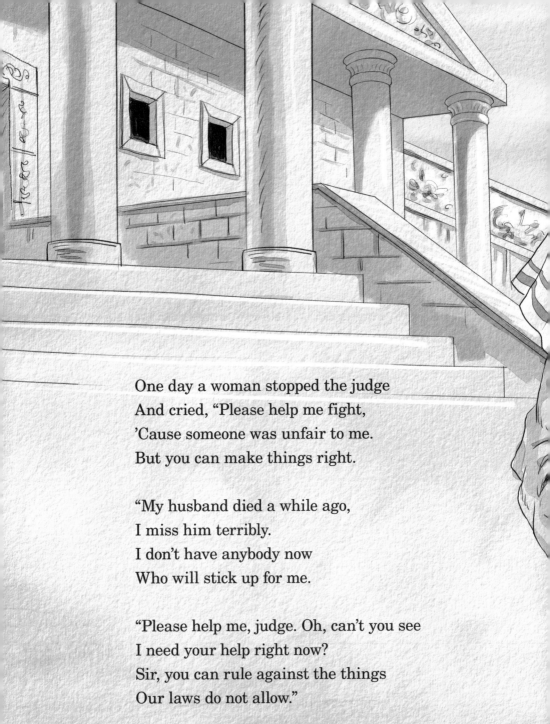

One day a woman stopped the judge
And cried, "Please help me fight,
'Cause someone was unfair to me.
But you can make things right.

"My husband died a while ago,
I miss him terribly.
I don't have anybody now
Who will stick up for me.

"Please help me, judge. Oh, can't you see
I need your help right now?
Sir, you can rule against the things
Our laws do not allow."

"Oh, go away," the judge replied.
"I have no time for you.
Your problems just don't matter—
I have better things to do."

The judge walked off. The woman left.
Her head was hanging low.
"All judges should be fair," she thought,
"How dare he just say no!"

"My life would be much better if
The judge ruled in my favor.
I won't give up," she told herself.
She started feeling braver.

Day after day, the woman stood
Outside the courthouse door.
And when the judge walked by, she called,
"What are you waiting for?

"I'll be here every day until
You do what's right for me!"
The judge said, "Stop your whining!
You're a bother, don't you see?"

But all her begging made him think,
"That woman's here to stay.
Each day I hope she won't come back,
But she won't go away.

"Her problems aren't important,
And I sure don't want to save her.
But I'm tired of her pestering,
So I'll rule in her favor."

Because the woman begged and begged,
She finally got her way.
Now why did Jesus tell this tale?
Here's what He had to say:

"That judge who was so slow to help
Was nothing like My Father.
God's pleased when people pray to Him;
It never is a bother.

"And if that wicked judge could do
A good thing after all,
Then how much more will God help
All His children big and small?"

Just like the woman, don't give up.
Pray often, every day.
God loves it when you talk to Him.
He hears all that you say.

Remember—stick to praying,
Just like paper sticks to glue.
Because God loves to hear from you,
That's something good to do.

Dear Parents,

This parable is about how God always listens to us because He loves us. Jesus wants us to understand that God is not at all like the selfish judge who thought only of himself and didn't want to be bothered by others' requests. The judge's attitude is in great contrast to God's love for His children.

Because God loves us so much, we like talking to Him. Jesus promises in this parable that God listens to our every word when we pray to Him. God wants us to talk to Him every day and never grow weary of it.

Encourage your child to talk to God anytime, both silently and aloud, to share wants, needs, and joys with Him. Help your child praise and thank Him in the morning, at mealtime, and at bedtime. Your child will also have opportunities to pray and sing hymns with Christian teachers, your minister, and members of your community of faith.

The wicked judge in the parable ended up doing a good thing, even though he did it for a selfish reason. Jesus reminds His disciples that if a nasty person like the judge could do what was right, then how much more will a loving God do what is right for His children?

As parents, you have a wonderful opportunity to guide your child to pray for things that Jesus prayed for, rather than for more toys and gadgets. The list below offers just a few of the things that can be added to children's prayers. You might also find prayer books for kids that are helpful for your child's prayer life.

- **Thank You, Jesus, for dying for me so that someday I will go to heaven. And thank You for forgiving my sins.**
- **Please be with _____ while he/she is sick and make _____ well soon.**
- **Thank You, God, for being everywhere, in my heart, in my home, and wherever I go, so I can talk to You anywhere and You'll hear me.**
- **Help me to obey You, especially when I'm thinking of doing something naughty.**
- **I'm in trouble, Lord. Please help me with _____.**
- **Please send Your holy angels to guard me and keep me from sin.**
- **Thank You for my food, my home, my parents, and everything You give me.**

The Author